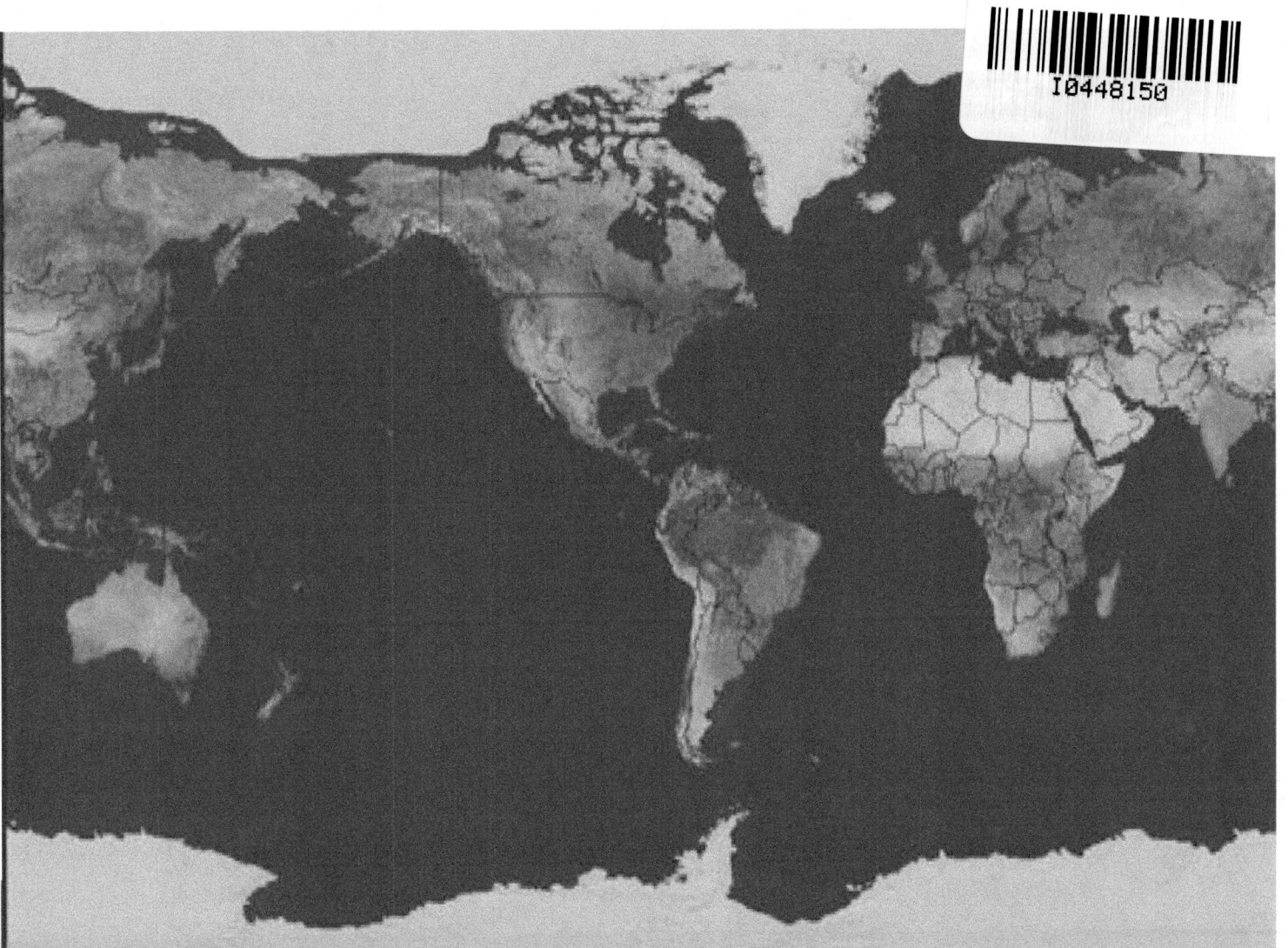

INTERNATIONAL OUTREACH AND COORDINATION STRATEGY

FOR
THE NATIONAL STRATEGY FOR MARITIME SECURITY

NOVEMBER 2005

United States Department of State

Washington, D.C.   20520

Message from the Secretary

Throughout our history as a nation, the great oceans, lakes, and rivers that surround and run through the United States have been vital to our prosperity and to our security. Today, we continue to depend on these maritime highways for a global transportation system that delivers goods and materials "just-in-time" to factories and stores across our country and around the world. The oceans and waterways are also critical sources of energy, minerals, food, and other natural resources, as well as favorite areas for recreation. Ships, submarines, and naval aviation remain key to our national defense.

For most of our history, warfare and perils such as piracy were first on our minds when we thought of threats to maritime security. Today, however, we also face a determined and resourceful terrorist enemy who would turn the vehicles of peaceful transportation – including ships, as well as planes, trains and trucks – into deadly instruments of destruction. This enemy will attack not only naval vessels like the *USS Cole*, but also commercial vessels such as the *M/V Limberg*, a French tanker.

A government has no higher duty than to protect its citizens. The President, therefore, has directed the preparation of *The National Strategy for Maritime Security* to "prevent the maritime domain from being used by terrorists, criminals, and hostile States to commit acts of terrorism, criminal or other unlawful or hostile acts against the United States, its people, economy, property, territory, allies, and friends." The President called for a fully coordinated United States government effort to safeguard our interests in the global maritime domain. The President required the inclusion of an *International Outreach and Coordination Strategy* as an integral part of the strategy, because a robust international effort is essential in achieving this objective,. As directed by the President, the *International Outreach and Coordination Strategy* focuses on (1) garnering international support for maritime security programs and initiatives that are central to an effective global maritime security framework and (2) enhancing international outreach efforts to ensure the security of the United States' interests in the Maritime domain.

The President charged the Department of State with leading the outreach effort to build and sustain alliances within the community of nations to help achieve the goal of a more secure world. At a time when global terrorism, rogue states, international crime and weapons of mass destruction threaten the world's oceans and waterways, no one nation can accomplish this goal alone. Success will come through the hard work of a powerful coalition of nations focused on protecting the world's maritime interests. The United States has a unique responsibility and opportunity to build cooperative relationships to defeat terrorists and criminal organizations, while protecting trade and legitimate maritime activities upon which the prosperity and security of the United States and our friends around the world depend.

Our own security and prosperity are best guaranteed when our international partners are also secure and prosperous. All nations benefit from effective global maritime security, and all nations must share in the responsibility of achieving this goal. With this *International Outreach and Coordination Strategy* as a guide, the men and women of the Department of State, in close coordination with other Departments and Agencies with authority and responsibility for maritime security, will enhance existing ties and forge new partnerships with other nations, international and regional organizations, and the private sector to improve global maritime security.

Condoleezza Rice
Secretary of State

FOREWORD

By signing National Security Presidential Directive 41/Homeland Security Presidential Directive 13 (NSPD-41/HSPD-13) President Bush underscored the importance of securing the maritime domain, which is defined as *"All areas and things of, on, under, relating to, adjacent to, or bordering on a sea, ocean, or other navigable waterway, including all maritime-related activities, infrastructure, people, cargo, and vessels and other conveyances."* NSPD-41/HSPD-13 established a Maritime Security Policy Coordinating Committee (MSPCC)—the first coordinating committee specifically tasked to address this issue—to oversee the development of a National Strategy for Maritime Security (NSMS) and eight supporting implementation plans:

- **The National Plan to Achieve Maritime Domain Awareness** lays the foundation for an effective understanding of anything associated with the maritime domain and identifying threats as early and as distant from our shores as possible.
- **The Global Maritime Intelligence Integration Plan** uses existing capabilities to integrate all available intelligence regarding potential threats to U.S. interests in the maritime domain.
- **The Maritime Operational Threat Response Plan** facilitates coordinated U.S. government response to threats against the United States and its interests in the maritime domain by establishing roles and responsibilities, which enable the government to respond quickly and decisively.
- **The International Outreach and Coordination Strategy** provides a framework to coordinate all maritime security initiatives undertaken with foreign governments and international organizations, and solicits international support for enhanced maritime security.
- **The Maritime Infrastructure Recovery Plan** recommends standardized procedures for restoration of maritime transportation systems following an incident of national significance.
- **Maritime Transportation System Security Recommendations** provide strategic context to holistically improve the security of the Marine Transportation System.
- **The Maritime Commerce Security Plan** establishes a comprehensive plan to secure the maritime supply chain.
- **The Domestic Outreach Plan** engages non-Federal input to assist with the development and implementation of maritime security policies resulting from NSPD-41/HSPD-13.

Although these plans address different aspects of maritime security, they are mutually linked and reinforce each other. Together, NSMS and its supporting plans represent the beginning of a comprehensive national effort to promote global economic stability and protect legitimate activities, while preventing hostile or illegal acts within the Maritime domain.

PREFACE

In accordance with National Security Presidential Directive NSPD-41 and Homeland Security Presidential Directive HSPD-13, the Secretary of State shall lead the coordination of the United States' international maritime security outreach efforts. The Department of State's *International Outreach and Coordination Strategy to Enhance Maritime Security* sets forth a plan to coordinate the United States' international outreach efforts regarding maritime security initiatives and to solicit international support for an improved global maritime security framework. *The International Outreach and Coordination Strategy* advances the policies set forth by President Bush in *The National Security Strategy, The National Strategy for Homeland Security,* and *The National Strategy for Maritime Security* and will help to accomplish the President's vision of a fully coordinated United States Government effort to protect our interests in the maritime domain.

TABLE OF CONTENTS

I. INTERNATIONAL OUTREACH AND COORDINATION STRATEGY TO ENHANCE MARITIME SECURITY

INTRODUCTION

The maritime domain encompasses trade routes, communication links, and natural resources vital to the global economy and the well-being of people in the United States and around the world. In today's globalized world, events beyond our borders have an undeniable impact on United States' interests. Attacks on ships, ports, or maritime transportation infrastructure by terrorists, rogue nations, or transnational criminal organizations can, within a frighteningly short time, produce terrible destruction and significantly disrupt the flow of international trade upon which we all depend. No one nation can single-handedly secure every ocean and every waterway around the world. Because the oceans play an indispensable role in the safety, security, and economic stability of the international community, all nations have a vital interest in ensuring that the Maritime domain remains secure and open for the free and legitimate use of all. Public and private entities must work in concert to succeed. Accordingly, in order to enhance global maritime security, the Department of State will leverage its diplomatic resources and influence, while coordinating closely with other components of the United States government, to promote and enhance close cooperation among sovereign nations, international and regional organizations, and the maritime private sector, including manufacturers, shippers, ship owners, seafarers, dockside workers, truckers, retailers, and recreational boaters.

II. STRATEGIC ENVIRONMENT: THE UNITED STATES – A MARITIME NATION IN A GLOBALIZED WORLD

Covering 70% of the Earth's surface, the world's oceans and waterways offer all nation-states a network of enormous importance to their security and prosperity. These sea-roads have been a primary driver in the globalization of commercial interests, allowing all nations to participate in the ever-expanding global marketplace. This maritime transportation system is vast, serving more than 100,000 ocean-going ships, as well as tens of millions of workboats, fishing vessels and recreational vessels. Every nation, including the United States, depends on an efficient and open maritime transportation system of waterways, ports, and intermodal connections to carry people and cargo to, from and along its shores. More than 40% of the world's merchant fleet enters United States harbors in any one year. Approximately 30,000 containers enter United States ports every day, and nearly 95% of all international commerce enters the United States through the nation's 361 public and private ports. Over 80% of the world's trade travels by water. The Maritime domain plays a critical role in the U.S. and global economies.

The United States now faces myriad non-traditional, asymmetric, and unpredictable threats from state and non-State actors, as well as from terrorist and transnational criminal organizations. Globalization has vastly increased the range and potential effects of such threats. Appendix A summarizes the major threats to the Maritime Domain. With more than 98,000 miles of shoreline and 3.5 million square miles of water within our exclusive economic zone (EEZ), the United States is particularly susceptible to attack from the maritime domain. The maritime domain presents a broad array of potential targets – such as piers, power or chemical plants, refineries, passenger terminals, military bases, bridges, locks, dams, and nearby facilities – that fit terrorists' objectives of inflicting mass casualties, major economic disruption, and significant psychological distress.

While the oceans' role as highways and facilitators of commerce grows, waterways have increasingly become both targets and conveyances for hostile, dangerous, and illicit activities. The openness that makes the maritime domain so important to international commerce also represents a great vulnerability. The vastness of the oceans, as well as the great length of shorelines, provides both concealment and numerous access points to land. Capitalizing on the relative ease and anonymity of movement by ship through the maritime domain, terrorists, criminal organizations, and rogue nations may smuggle or attempt to smuggle weapons of mass destruction, conventional arms, narcotics, and human beings. Where possible, they may use legitimate maritime business as fronts for these activities. Because two-thirds of the world's people live within 240 miles of a seacoast,[1] large numbers of people are potentially subject to threats from these groups that exploit the maritime domain.

An attack on a strategic point in the maritime domain, such as the Panama Canal, the locks of the St. Lawrence Seaway, or the Suez Canal, could devastate people and economies worldwide. The disruption of cross-border cargo deliveries to the United States following the attacks of September 11, 2001, and the closure of West Coast ports during a major labor dispute in 2002, underscore the vital role that international trade and transport play in the United States and world economy. It has been estimated that the West Coast port shutdown cost the United States economy billions of dollars. The Brookings Institute has estimated that a weapon of mass destruction or effect[2] hidden in a container or in the mail could cause damage and disruption costing the United States economy as much as one trillion dollars.[3]

The United States is not alone in recognizing the vital importance of securing the maritime domain. Other nations have also begun to focus on the importance of maritime security. An effective global maritime security framework that harmonizes free trade and maritime security will uphold sovereignty, strengthen economies, enhance international partnerships, and secure the maritime domain from terrorism and other unlawful or hostile acts.

---

[1] Bryant, D. Rodenburg, E., Cox, T. And Nielsen, D. Coastlines at Risk: An index of potential development-related threats to coastal ecosystems. Washington, D.C., World Resources Institute, 1995. (WRI Indicator Brief)
[2] The term "weapon of mass destruction / effect" or WMD/E refers to a broad range of adversary capabilities that pose potentially devastating effects. WMD/E includes chemical, biological, radiological, nuclear, and enhanced high explosive weapons.
[3] Michael E. O'Hanton et al., Protecting the American Homeland: A Preliminary Analysis, Washington, D.C.: Brookings Institute Press, 2002

III. STRATEGIC GOALS

To safeguard the maritime domain, the United States must forge cooperative partnerships and alliances with other nations, as well as with public and private stakeholders in the international community. We cannot and should not attempt to patrol every coastline, inspect every ship, screen every passenger, or peer into every container crossing the world's oceans. To foster stronger partnerships within the international community, the United States must have a coordinated and consistent approach to building international support and cooperation to reinforce global maritime security. We will propose ideas, and encourage others to do the same. We will speak frankly. We will also listen carefully. We will work together. Security must be a team effort.

Consistent with National Security Presidential Directive NSPD-41 and Homeland Security Presidential Directive HSPD-13, this *Strategy* establishes the following <u>Strategic Goals</u>:

- A *coordinated policy* for United States government maritime security activities with foreign governments, international and regional organizations, and the private sector.
- *Enhanced outreach* to foreign governments, international and regional organizations, private sector partners, and the public abroad to solicit support for improved global maritime security.

The United States recognizes the inherent right of every nation, including our own, to defend itself, to protect its legitimate national interests, and to prevent unlawful exploitation of the maritime domain. The United States will foster cooperation within the international community through diplomacy and mutual assistance. The United States will also, when necessary, take all appropriate actions, consistent with U.S. and international law, to defend ourselves, our allies, and our national interests around the world.

IV. STRATEGIC INTENT

The National Strategy for Maritime Security, along with its associated eight national plans,[4] represents a multi-layered approach and includes increased maritime domain awareness[5] as well as enhanced prevention, protection, and recovery capabilities. We will continue to strengthen our ability to detect and deter illicit activities in the maritime domain, to defend ourselves and our allies, and to recover from or to assist others in recovering from any terrorist or hostile act against U.S. interests or the interests of our allies or key trading partners. We will do so by enlisting the cooperation and support of our allies and partners, both public and private, throughout the world.

The United States' approach to ensuring the security and safety of the maritime domain, including maritime-related activities, infrastructure, people, cargo, and vessels – like the maritime sector itself – is broad, taking advantage of all aspects of United States influence, including diplomatic, military, law enforcement, and regulatory efforts. We will promote global maritime security based on the rule of law, enforced by sovereign states, and supported by international and regional organizations, as well as the private sector. The goal is to protect international trade, economic cooperation, and legitimate maritime activities of all kinds. To achieve this goal, we will cooperate and collaborate with other governments, international and regional organizations, international business, and all those who work on, depend on, or use the maritime domain.

---

[4] International Outreach and Coordination Strategy to Enhance Maritime Security, National Maritime Domain Awareness Plan, Maritime Operational Threat Response Plan, Maritime Infrastructure Recovery Plan, Maritime Transportation System Security Plan, Maritime Commerce Security Plan, Global Maritime Intelligence Integration Plan, and the Domestic Outreach Plan

[5] "Maritime Domain Awareness" is defined as the effective understanding of anything associated with the global maritime domain that could impact the security, safety, economy, or environment of the United States.

V. STRATEGIC EXECUTION AND OBJECTIVES

The Department of State, in close coordination with other Departments and Agencies in the United States Government with responsibilities and authorities for security of the maritime domain, will lead active international outreach and engagement to enhance global maritime security. These efforts will be aligned with domestic outreach efforts and activities to ensure the development of consistent messages and materials. Comprehensive security of the maritime domain must be approached in partnership not only with foreign governments and international organizations, but also with the international business community that relies upon security and efficiency in the movement of vessels, people, and goods. The United States will continue to explore new avenues and opportunities for outreach and cooperation both domestically and internationally, as well as support and expand upon the work that has already begun in this critical area of our national security efforts.

The United States will seek early dialogue with international partners when developing maritime security policy initiatives, and will maintain regular contact to discuss implementation and ensure effectiveness. The goal is mutually supportive policies, focused on keeping maritime systems secure and recognizing that a variety of approaches, based on different physical circumstances as well as different political, legal, and economic institutions, may foster security of the maritime domain. We will work continuously in the United States and abroad to identify best practices and to communicate them to others, reflecting the priorities of the United States and our partners.

Foreign governments and industry officials will be provided clear and consistent United States government positions on programs and initiatives related to maritime security, as coordinated through the Maritime Security Policy Coordinating Committee. Appendix B lists ongoing United States Government maritime security initiatives. This annex will be updated regularly, to reflect the latest United States maritime security policies and initiatives. Appendix C lists international, regional and industry organizations that support efforts to enhance maritime security in the international community and with which the United States will continue to work closely in advancing global maritime security.

In order to achieve the <u>Strategic Goals</u> of this *International Outreach and Coordination Strategy*, the Department of State (through the Office of Transportation Policy in the Bureau of Economic and Business Affairs and the Office of Oceans Affairs in the Bureau of Oceans and International Environmental and Scientific Affairs), in close coordination with all U.S. government components with equities in securing the maritime domain, will pursue the following <u>Strategic Objectives</u>:

Strategic Goal: A *coordinated policy* for United States government maritime security activities with foreign governments, international and regional organizations, and the private sector.

- **Strategic Objective**: Establish unified, consistent U.S. positions on maritime security programs and initiatives for U.S. bilateral and multilateral exchanges.

- **Strategic Objective**: Emphasize the importance of maritime security as a key priority in U.S. international policy.

- **Strategic Objective**: Ensure the full integration of international law in the advancement of global maritime security at international meetings and exchanges.

- **Strategic Objective**: Optimize the use of meetings and other exchanges with countries, international and regional organizations, and private sector groups to advance maritime security.

Strategic Goal: *Enhanced outreach* to foreign governments, international and regional organizations, private sector partners, and the public abroad to solicit support for improved global maritime security.

- **Strategic Objective**: Build partnerships with other countries and the maritime community to identify and reach out to regional and international organizations in order to advance global maritime security.

- **Strategic Objective**: Coordinate U.S. and international technical assistance to promote effective maritime security in developing nations and critical regions.

- **Strategic Objective**: Coordinate a unified message on maritime security for public diplomacy.

- **Strategic Objective**: Provide U.S missions abroad with guidance to enable them to build support for U.S. maritime security initiatives with host governments, key private-sector partners, and the general public abroad.

VI. Conclusion

The security of the maritime domain is a global issue. The United States is committed to working closely with our allies and partners around the world to ensure that lawful private and public activities in the maritime domain are protected against attack and criminal or otherwise unlawful or hostile exploitation. Our allies and trading partners recognize the importance the United States places on maritime security, and we will work closely with them to develop effective international maritime security programs. The United States will continue to expand our working partnerships with all who share the goal of a secure and prosperous international trading community. Many Departments and Agencies of the United States government share the challenge of engaging our allies and partners, as well as working with appropriate international and regional organizations and private sector groups in order to secure United States maritime interests around the globe. The Department of State will coordinate with and support other Departments and Agencies in developing and communicating to foreign partners a unified and consistent message regarding global maritime security and United States maritime security programs and initiatives.

APPENDIX A: THREATS TO THE MARITIME DOMAIN

The National Strategy for Maritime Security details the threats posed to the maritime domain. The explanation of these threats is repeated below for convenience.

Section II Threats to Maritime Security

"America, in this new century, again faces new threats. Instead of massed armies, we face stateless networks; we face killers who hide in our own cities. We must confront deadly technologies. To inflict great harm on our country, America's enemies need to be only right once. Our intelligence and law enforcement professionals in our government must be right every single time."

> President Bush
>
> Washington, D.C.
>
> 17 December 2004

Complexity and ambiguity are hallmarks of today's security environment, especially in the maritime domain. In addition to the potential for major combat operations at sea, terrorism has dramatically increased the nature of non-military, transnational and asymmetric threats in the maritime domain that the United States and its allies and strategic partners must be prepared to counter. Unlike traditional military scenarios in which adversaries and theaters of action are clearly defined, these nonmilitary, transnational threats often demand more than purely military undertakings to be defeated.

Unprecedented advances in telecommunications and dramatic improvements in international commercial logistics have combined to increase both the range and effects of such illegal activities, providing the physical means to transcend even the most secure borders and to move rapidly across great distances. Adversaries that take advantage of such transnational capabilities have the potential to cause serious damage to global, political, and economic security. The maritime domain in particular presents not only a medium by which these threats can move, but offers a broad array of potential targets that fit the terrorists' operational objectives of achieving mass casualties and inflicting catastrophic economic harm. While the variety of actors threatening the maritime domain continues to grow in number and capability, they can be broadly grouped as nation-states, terrorists, and transnational criminals and pirates. Defeating the threat of the widely dispersed terrorist networks that present an immediate danger to U.S. national security interests at home and abroad remains our foremost objective.

Nation-State Threats

The prospect of major regional conflicts erupting, escalating, and drawing in major powers should not be discounted. Nonetheless, in the absence of inter-state conflict, individual state actions represent a more significant challenge to global security. Some states provide safe havens for criminals and terrorists, who use these countries as bases of operations to export illegal activities into the maritime domain and into other areas of the globe. The probability of a hostile state using a weapon of mass destruction (WMD) is expected to increase during the next decade[6]. An alternative danger is that a foreign state will provide critical advanced conventional weaponry, WMD components, delivery systems and related materials, technologies, and weapons expertise to another rogue state or a terrorist organization that is willing to conduct WMD attacks. WMD issues are of the greatest concern since the maritime domain is the likely venue by which WMD will be brought into the United States.

Terrorist Threats

Non-state terrorist groups that exploit open borders challenge the sovereignty of nations and have an increasingly damaging effect on international affairs. With advanced telecommunications, they can coordinate their actions among dispersed cells while remaining in the shadows. Successful attacks in the maritime domain provide opportunities to cause significant disruption to regional and global economies. Today's terrorists are increasing their effectiveness and reach by establishing links with other like-minded organizations around the globe. Some terrorists groups have used shipping as a means of conveyance for positioning their agents, logistical support, and generating revenue. Terrorists have also taken advantage of criminal smuggling networks to circumvent border security measures.

Terrorists have indicated a strong desire to use WMD.[7] This prospect creates a more complex and perilous security situation, further aggravated by countries that are unable to account for or adequately secure their stockpiles of such weapons and associated materials. This circumstance, coupled with increased access to the technology needed to build and employ those weapons, increases the possibility that a terrorist attack involving WMD could occur. Similarly, bioterrorism appears particularly suited to use by smaller but sophisticated groups because this tactic is exceedingly difficult to detect in comparison to other mass-effects weapons.

Terrorists can also develop effective attack capabilities relatively quickly using a variety of platforms, including explosives-laden suicide boats[8] and light aircraft; merchant and cruise ships as kinetic weapons to ram another vessel, warship, port facility, or offshore platform; commercial vessels as launch platforms for missile attacks; underwater swimmers to infiltrate ports; and unmanned underwater explosive delivery vehicles. Mines are also an effective weapon because they are low cost, readily available, easily deployed, difficult to counter and require minimal training. Terrorists can also take

---

[6] Mapping the Global Future, National Intelligence Council, Washington, DC: December 2004.
[7] *The National Security Strategy of the United States of America*, p.15.
[8] This maritime mode of terrorist attack has been established, tested, and repeated. The terrorist group al-Qaida in October 2000 successfully attacked the *USS Cole* in Yemen with an explosives-laden suicide small boat and 2 years later attacked the French oil tanker *M/V Limburg*.

advantage of a vessel's legitimate cargo, such as chemicals, petroleum, or liquefied natural gas, as the explosive component of an attack. Vessels can be used to transport powerful conventional explosives or WMD for detonation in a port or alongside an offshore facility.

The U.S. economy and national security are fully dependent upon information technology and the information infrastructure.[9] Terrorists might attempt cyber attacks to disrupt critical information networks or attempt to cause physical damage to information systems that are integral to the operation of marine transportation and commerce systems. Tools and methodologies for attacking information systems are becoming widely available, and the technical abilities and sophistication of terrorists groups bent on causing havoc or disruption is increasing.

> However, the nature and motivations of these new adversaries, their determination to obtain destructive powers hitherto available only to the world's strongest states, and the greater likelihood that they will use weapons of mass destruction against us, make today's security environment more complex and dangerous.
>
> Prevent Our Enemies from Threatening Us, Our Allies, and Our Friends
> with Weapons of Mass Destruction
> Goal V of the National Security Strategy of the United States

Transnational Criminal and Piracy Threats

The continued growth in legitimate international commerce in the maritime domain has been accompanied by growth in the use of the maritime domain for criminal purposes. The smuggling of people, drugs, weapons, and other contraband, as well as piracy and armed robbery against vessels, pose a threat to maritime security. Piracy and incidents of maritime crime tend to be concentrated in areas of heavy commercial maritime activity, especially where there is significant political and economic instability, or in regions with little or no maritime law enforcement capacity. Today's pirates and criminals are usually well organized and well equipped with advanced communications, weapons, and high-speed craft. The capabilities to board and commandeer large underway vessels - demonstrated in numerous piracy incidents - could also be employed to facilitate terrorist acts.

Just as the world's oceans are avenues for a nation's overseas commerce, they are also the highways for the import or export of illegal commodities. Maritime drug trafficking[10] generates vast amounts of money for international organized crime syndicates and terrorist organizations. Laundered through the international financial system, this money provides a huge source of virtually untraceable funds. These monetary assets can then be used to bribe government officials, bypass established financial controls, and fund additional illegal activities, including arms trafficking, migrant smuggling, and terrorist

---

[9] The *National Strategy to Secure Cyberspace* is part of our overall effort to protect the Nation. It is an implementing component of the *National Strategy for Homeland Security* and is complemented by a *National Strategy for the Physical Protection of Critical Infrastructures and Key Assets.*
[10] The *National Drug Control Strategy* outlines U.S. goals in this area.

operations. Further, these activities can ensure a steady supply of weapons and cash for terrorist operatives, as well as the means for their clandestine movement.

Environmental Destruction

Intentional acts that result in environmental disasters can have far-reaching, negative effects on the economic viability and political stability of a region. Additionally, in recent years, competition for declining marine resources has resulted in a number of violent confrontations as some of the world's fishers resort to unlawful activity. These incidents underscore the high stakes for the entire world as diminishing resources, such as fish stocks, put increasing pressure on maritime nations to undertake more aggressive actions. These actions continue to have the potential to cause conflict and regional instability. Similarly, massive pollution of the oceans, whether caused by terrorists or individuals who undertake intentional acts in wanton disregard for the consequences, could result in significant damage to ecosystems and undermine the national and economic security of the nations that depend on them.

Illegal Seaborne Migration

International migration is a long-standing issue that will remain a major challenge to regional stability, and it will be one of the most important factors affecting maritime security through the next 10 years. Transnational migration, spurred by a decline of social well-being or internal political unrest, has become common over the past decades. It will continue to drive the movement of many people, with the potential to upset regional stability because of the strain migrants and refugees place on fragile economies and political systems. In some countries the collapse of political and social order prompts maritime mass migrations, such as the ones the United States has experienced from Cuba and Haiti. The humanitarian and enforcement efforts entailed by the management of such migrations require a significant commitment of security resources.

The potential for terrorists to take advantage of human smuggling networks in attempts to circumvent border security measures cannot be ignored. As security in our ports of entry, at land-border crossings, and at airports continues to tighten, criminals and terrorists will likely consider our relatively undefended coastlines to be less risky alternatives for unlawful entry into the United States.

APPENDIX B: U.S. GOVERNMENT MARITIME SECURITY INITIATIVES – JULY 2005

The United States Government takes a layered and cooperative approach to maritime security, utilizing the expertise of federal, state and local authorities as well as that of the private sector and of international partners to create a system of security measures to protect one end of a sea-based journey to the other. The goal is to harmonize security measures and economic growth.

The layered, often interlocked or interrelated, security measures are designed to make it harder for terrorists or transnational criminal groups to attack the United States or harm our interests. These layered measures seek to protect the three phases of the maritime commerce chain -- overseas, in transit, and on U.S. shores. Following is an overview of the current maritime security programs and initiatives.

A. Overseas

Advance Electronic Cargo Information (24-Hour Rule)
www.cbp.gov/xp/cgov/import/communications_to_industry/advance_info

To evaluate the terrorist risks from sea cargo arriving and departing the United States, U.S. Customs and Border Protection (CBP) requires that all sea carriers provide information necessary to ensure cargo safety and security pursuant to those laws enforced and administered by CBP, before cargo arrives in the United States. Cargo information for containerized and break-bulk shipments must be received through the CBP Sea Automated Manifest System 24 hours prior to loading the cargo aboard the ship in the foreign port. Cargo information for bulk shipments must be received by CBP 24 hours prior to arrival of the ship in the United States. Failure to meet the Required Advance Electronic Cargo Information Rule will result in a "Do Not Load" message, denial of unlading in the United States for the vessel, and other penalties.

Contact: Department of Homeland Security/Customs and Border Protection/Office of Field Operations
Phone: 202-344-1320
Fax: 202-344-2777
Email: manifest.branch@dhs.gov
Website:
http://www.cbp.gov/xp/cgov/import/communications_to_industry/advance_info

Container Security Initiative (CSI)
http://www.cbp.gov/xp/cgov/border_security/international_csi/

The Container Security Initiative (CSI) is an initiative that was developed by U.S. Customs and Border Protection (CBP), in the aftermath of the terrorist attacks of September 11. The primary purpose of CSI is to protect the global trading system and the trade lanes between CSI ports and the United States. Under the CSI program, a team of officers is deployed to work with host nation counterparts to target all containers that pose a potential threat. Announced in January 2002, CSI was first implemented in the ports shipping the greatest volume of containers to the United States. CBP has entered into bilateral discussions with all the foreign governments where these top ports are located and is now expanding to additional ports in strategic locations.

The four core elements of CSI:
(1) using intelligence and automated information to identify and target containers that pose a risk for terrorism;
(2) pre-screening those containers that pose a risk at the port of departure before they arrive at U.S. ports;
(3) using detection technology to quickly pre-screen containers that pose a risk; and,
(4) using smarter, tamper-evident containers.

Contact: Department of Homeland Security/Customs and Border Protection/Office of International affairs/Container Security Initiative Division
Phone: 202-344-3040
Fax: 202-344-2040
E-mail: containersecurity@dhs.gov
Website: http://www.cbp.gov/xp/cgov/border_security/international_csi/

The Megaports Initiative
www.nnsa.doe.gov/na-20/sld.shtml

Under this program, the Department of Energy's National Nuclear Security Administration installs radiation detection equipment in the world's largest and busiest ports to help detect, deter, and interdict illicitly trafficked nuclear and other radioactive materials through the global maritime system before they reach U.S. shores. This program also provides training to host government officials in the operation and maintenance of the equipment. The program provides technical resources to complement the Container Security Initiative (CSI). The Megaports Initiative has installed monitoring systems in the Netherlands and Greece, and is installing equipment in the Bahamas, Belgium, Singapore, Spain, and Sri Lanka.

Contact: The Department of Energy/National Nuclear Security Administration/William Kilmartin
Phone: 202-586-0513
E-mail: William.Kilmartin@nnsa.doe.gov
Website: http://www.nnsa.doe.gov/na-20/sld.shtml

Transshipment Country Export Control Initiative (TECI)

TECI seeks to prevent the proliferation of weapons of mass destruction and the illicit diversion of sensitive U.S.-origin technology through global transshipment hubs. TECI works cooperatively with transshipment hub governments to strengthen export control systems and prevent improper re-exports and transshipments of U.S.-origin items. It also reaches out to the transportation industry to strengthen private trade compliance efforts through the adoption of best practices and other efforts. By doing so, TECI seeks to enhance security and confidence in international trade flows. As part of TECI, the Bureau of Industry and Security of the Department of Commerce has posted export control attaches in certain transshipment hubs, including the United Arab Emirates and Hong Kong, to work with host governments and local transportation firms.

Contact: Bureau of Industry and Security, Department of Commerce/Ajay Kuntamukkala
Phone: 202-482-1458
E-mail: akuntmu@bis.doc.gov
Website: http://www.bis.doc.gov/ComplianceAndEnforcement/ExecutiveSummary.html

Export Control and Related Border Security Assistance (EXBS)
http://www.state.gov/t/np/export/ecc/20779.htm

EXBS is a U.S. government interagency program managed by the Department of State. It seeks to prevent proliferation of weapons of mass destruction by assisting foreign governments establish and implement effective export control systems that meet international standards.

Drawing on the expertise from the Departments of State, Homeland Security, Commerce, Energy, Defense, and the private sector, the EXBS program has helped countries around the world improve their ability to prevent and interdict shipments of dangerous items and technology by providing a wide variety of practical assistance tailored to each individual country's needs.

Contact: Department of State /Office of Export Control Cooperation
Phone: 202-647-1675
Website: http://www.state.gov/t/np/export/ecc/20779.htm
E-mail: CrouchKF@state.gov

Proliferation Security Initiative (PSI)
http://www.state.gov/t/np/c10390.htm

The PSI, announced by President Bush on May 31, 2003, seeks to stop shipments of weapons of mass destruction (WMD), their delivery systems, and related materials to and from States and non-State actors worldwide. In September 2003, 11 countries committed to and published the PSI Statement of Interdiction Principles, which identifies specific steps for effectively interdicting such WMD-related shipments and preventing proliferation facilitators from engaging in WMD-related trafficking. Since then more than 60 countries have indicated their support for PSI, and 19 countries are actively participating in the PSI Operational Experts Group (OEG).

Contact for PSI diplomatic outreach: Department of State/Thomas D. Lehrman
Phone: 202-647-0069
Website: http://www.state.gov/t/np/c10390.htm
E-mail: LehrmanTD@state.gov

Regional Maritime Security Initiative (RMSI)

RMSI, jointly coordinated by Pacific Command and the U.S. Department of State, is a capacity-building program focused on enhancing cooperative security and maritime law enforcement capabilities in the East Asia and Pacific region, with an initial focus on the Malacca Straits. The Initiative is designed to increase maritime situational awareness through enhanced information gathering and sharing, not only among maritime agencies within a State, but also between States. It also aims to enhance effective decision-making procedures and interdiction skills.

Contact: U.S. Department of State /EAP/FO/Steve McGann
Phone: 202-647-7953
E-mail: McGannCS@state.gov

Maritime Transportation Security Act (MTSA) and the International Ship and Port Facility Security (ISPS) Code
www.uscg.mil/hq/g-m/mp/mtsa.shtml

Under the Maritime Transportation Security Act, the U.S. Coast Guard verifies the compliance of foreign ports and flag states vessels with the ISPS Code, which was adopted by the International Maritime Organization in December 2002 and came into force on July 1, 2004. The ISPS Code is a comprehensive, mandatory security regime, comprised of both mandatory and recommendatory components, for international shipping and port operations. It requires vessels and port facilities to conduct security assessments, develop security plans and hire security officers. It seeks to provide a standardized, consistent framework for evaluating risk, enabling governments to ensure that security measures are implemented in proportion to the potential risk to security, which may vary from time to time.

Contact: Department of Homeland Security/U.S. Coast Guard
For Ports: International Port Assessments/CDR Joseph LoSciuto
Phone: 202-366 1497
Fax: 202-366-1456
Email: jlosciuto@msc.uscg.mil

For Vessels: Foreign Vessel Compliance/LCDR Jason Neubauer
Phone 202-267-1406
Fax: 202- 267-0506
E-mail: jneubauer@comdt.uscg.mil
Website: http://www.uscg.mil/hq/g-m/mp/mtsa.shtml

International Port Security Program
www.uscg.mil/hq/g-m/mp/mtsa.shtml

Under this program, the U.S. Coast Guard and host nations work jointly to evaluate the countries' overall compliance with the ISPS Code. The U.S. Coast Guard uses the information gained from these visits to improve the United States' own security practices and to determine if additional security precautions will be required for vessels arriving in the United States from other countries.

Contact: Department of Homeland Security/U.S. Coast Guard/International Port Assessments/ CDR Joseph LoSciuto
Phone: 202-366 1497
Fax: 202-366-1456
E-mail: jlosciuto@msc.uscg.mil
Website: http://www.uscg.mil/hq/g-m/mp/mtsa.shtml

Customs – Trade Partnership Against Terrorism (C-TPAT)
www.cbp.gov/xp/cgov/import/commercial_enforcement/ctpat/

C-TPAT is a voluntary partnership between CBP and industry to secure the international supply chain from end to end. C-TPAT importers and other industry leaders secure supply chains from the foreign factory loading docks of their vendors to the port of arrival in the U.S. In turn, CBP offers C-TPAT shipments expedited processing and provides C-TPAT participants with other benefits.

In order to join C-TPAT, a company must conduct a self-assessment of its current supply chain security procedures using C-TPAT security criteria and best practices developed in partnership with logistics and security experts from the trade. A participant must commit to increasing its supply chain security to meet minimal supply chain security criteria. It must also commit to working with its business partners and customers throughout their supply chains to ensure that those businesses also increase their supply chain security.

Contact: Department of Homeland Security/Customs and Border Protection/Office of Field Operation
Phone: 202-344-1180; fax: 202-344-2626
E-mail: industry.partnership@dhs.gov
Website: http://www.cbp.gov/xp/cgov/import/commercial_enforcement/ctpat/

U.S. Coast Guard International Training Programs

The Coast Guard International Training Division (ITD) from Training Center Yorktown deploys teams worldwide and each fiscal year trains over 2000 international students in over 65 countries on Coast Guard missions, including maritime security related topics. Training is coordinated with the host nation and with the respective U.S. Embassy. Primary sources of funding include programs such as Department of State International

Narcotics and Law Enforcement Affairs (INL), or Security Assistance Programs of International Military Education and Training (IMET), the Regional Defense Counter Terrorism Fellowship Program (RDCTFP), Foreign Military Financing (FMF), and Foreign Military Sales (FMS).

The Coast Guard ITD also includes the International Maritime Officer School, which provides maritime law enforcement and maritime security training to international students. In addition, there are three courses designed especially for international officers: the International Maritime Officer Course (IMOC), the International Crisis Command and Control Course (ICCC), and the International Leadership and Management Seminar (ILAMS).

Exportable International Training
Contact: CDR Matt Creelman
E-mail: mcreelman@tcyorktown.uscg.mil
Phone: 757-856-2295
Contact: LCDR Charles Caruolo (G-CI)
Phone: 202-267-2555
E-mail: ccaruolo@comdt.uscg.mil

Asia-Pacific Economic Cooperation (APEC) Forum
www.apec.org/apec.html

The U.S. government works in APEC, comprising 21 economies on the Pacific Rim, to facilitate trade and investment and enhance security against terrorist threats. Member economies have agreed to: implement a container security regime; implement the common standards for electronic customs reporting developed by the World Customs Organization; promote private-sector adoption of supply chain security; and assure integrity of officials involved in border operations.

Contact: U.S. Customs and Border Protection/Eileen McLucas
Phone: 202-344-3553
E-mail: eileen.mclucas@dhs.gov

The U.S. government also works with APEC in assisting its member economies to implement the International Ship and Port Facility Security Code, through training, technical assistance, and capacity-building programs.

Contact: Department of Homeland Security/Transportation Security Administration/Patrick Burns
Phone: 571-227-1223
E-mail: Patrick.Burns@dhs.gov
Website: http://www.apec.org/apec.html

Group of Eight (G8)
www.g8.gov.uk

Within the G8 Lyon-Roma Group, the United States has developed a methodology and checklist for the auditing of port and maritime security. This proposal has been adopted by the International Maritime Organization as an international self-assessment checklist.

Contact: Department of State/INL/PC/Scott Harris
Phone: 202-647-0458
E-mail: HarrisST@state.gov
Website: http://www.g8.gov.uk

Organization of American States (OAS)
www.oas.org/cip/defaulte.asp

The U.S. Maritime Administration (MARAD), the Department of Homeland Security, and the U.S. Permanent Mission to the OAS help OAS member states enhance passenger and cargo security at their ports through the Inter-American Port Security Training Program. By helping them comply with the International Shipping and Port Security Code and related security agreements, this program improves the safety of American citizens and shippers. It reduces the vulnerability of regional ports and cruise ships to terrorist attack and of shippers to the threat of unconventional weapons being placed in their containers. (Through the Maritime Transportation Act of 2002, the U.S. Congress stipulated that the MARAD/OAS Inter-American Port Security Training Program be the model for international training.)

Contact: Department of State/U.S. Mission to the OAS/Sergio Garcia
Phone: 202-647-9914
E-mail: garciasa2@state.gov
Website: http://www.oas.org/cip/defaulte.asp

Enduring Friendship

Enduring Friendship is a U.S. Southern Command (SOUTHCOM) initiative focused on accomplishing three of SOUTHCOM's four main Theater Strategy elements in the Caribbean, Central and South America - building regional cooperative security; developing roles and missions for the 21st century; and, supporting the national counter-terrorism/drug policy. Enduring Friendship is a voluntary program aimed at synchronizing multinational operational maritime forces of the Americas to assist with security against transnational and asymmetrical maritime threats, such as drug and weapon trafficking, terrorism, uncontrolled migration, fish poaching and other threats to maritime life, hazards to navigation, and humanitarian emergencies. Two major changes that Enduring Friendship seeks to enact are a reduced pressure on U.S. assets in the Caribbean Basin and expanding the maritime capabilities of our partner nations to make them more self- and mutually-reliant.

Contact: SOUTHCOM CDR Ike Clark
Phone: 305-437-1516
E-mail: clarkw@hq.southcom.mil

B. In Transit

Operation Safe Commerce (OSC)

Operation Safe Commerce (OSC) is the Department of Homeland Security's (DHS) primary supply chain security test and deployment program. It is a partnership between the U.S. government, the three largest U.S. container ports (ports of Los Angeles and Long Beach, ports of Seattle and Tacoma and the Port Authority of New York/New Jersey) and the maritime industry. Its goal is to improve the security of containerized cargo movements by testing commercial technology and business process solutions. It is a critical component of DHS' efforts in cargo security.

The Department of Homeland Security's Office of State and Local Government Coordination and Preparedness (SLGCP), Office of Domestic Preparedness manages, monitors and provides support to the Operation Safe Commerce program in coordination with an interagency executive steering committee (Departments of Transportation, State and Commerce; United States Coast Guard, United States Customs and Border Protection, Border and Transportation Security Directorate; and the Transportation Security Administration).

Operation Safe Commerce does not conflict or impinge upon any existing governmental initiatives. It is a government sponsored cooperative agreement grant program established to provide a test bed to examine methods to improve supply chain security. This public-private partnership does not impose either voluntary or mandatory practices or regulations on industry. Its intent, in part, is to assist in identifying best practices in supply chain security. Operation Safe Commerce is a finite project.

Contact: Department of Homeland Security/Transportation Security Administration/Ken Concepcion
Phone: 202-786-9512
E-mail: kenneth.concepcion@dhs.gov

Smart Box Initiative

The Smart Box technology involves an imbedded, electronic container security device that helps U.S. authorities to determine whether a container has been opened or tampered with at any point along its journey.

Contact: Department of Homeland Security/Customs and Border Protection/Office of Field Operations
Phone: 202-344-1180
Fax: 202-344-1435

The Automated Targeting System (ATS)

With input from the intelligence community, Customs and Border Protection (CBP) uses this rules-based system to perform transactional risk assessments and evaluate potential national security risks posed by cargo and passengers before they arrive in the United States.

Contact: Department of Homeland Security/Customs and Border Protection/Office of Field Operations
Phone: 202-344-1180
Fax: 202-344-1435

96-Hour Advance Notice of Arrival
www.uscg.mil/hq/g-m/mp/mtsa.shtml

In order to determine which vessels require additional attention, including at-sea boarding or escort during transits of U.S. waters, the U.S. Coast Guard requires that all ships provide detailed information on the crew, passenger, cargo, and voyage history 96 hours before arriving in a U.S. port. In addition to analyzing this information, the U.S. Coast Guard reviews previous security problems with the vessel or illegal activity on the part of the crew, as well as the security environment in previous ports of call.

Contact: Department of Homeland Security/U.S. Coast Guard/LT Craig Toomey
Phone: 202-267-0476
Fax: 202-267-0506
E-mail: cstoomey@comdt.uscg.mil
Website: http://www.uscg.mil/hq/g-m/mp/mtsa.shtml

Advance Passenger Information System Rule (APIS)

In April 2005, CBP published a final APIS rule which requires all commercial vessels to submit electronic crewmember and passenger manifests up to 96 hours in advance of arrival into, and 15 minutes in advance of departure from, the United States. These electronic manifests are vetted through law enforcement databases that include the terrorists watch lists. This rule allows the Department of Homeland Security to identify known/suspected terrorists prior to their arrival and departure from the U.S. It also supports U.S. Coast Guard analysis with its 96-Hour Rule.

Contact: Department of Homeland Security/Customs and Border Protection/Office of Field Operations
Phone: 202-344-1180
Fax: 202-344-1435

Ship Security Alert System (SSAS)
www.uscg.mil/hq/g-m/mp/mtsa.shtml

SSAS allows a vessel operator to send a covert alert to shore for incidents involving acts of violence, such as piracy or terrorism. The International Ship and Port Facility Security Code requires new passenger and cargo ships of at least 500 gross tons to install this equipment by July 1, 2004. Existing passenger vessels and cargo vessels must have the equipment installed prior to the first radio survey after July 1, 2004, or by July 1, 2006. Other types of vessels may carry and use SSAS voluntarily.

Contact: Department of Homeland Security/U.S. Coast Guard/LT Craig Toomey
Phone: 202-267 0476
Fax: 202-267-0506
E-mail: cstoomey@comdt.uscg.mil
Website: http://www.uscg.mil/hq/g-m/mp/mtsa.shtml

Public Health Security and Bioterrorism Preparedness and Response Act of 2002 (The Bioterrorism Act)
www.fda.gov/oc/bioterrorism/bioact.html

This act requires that the U.S. Food and Drug Administration (FDA) receive prior notification of all FDA regulated human and animal food, as well as dietary supplements imported or offered for import to the United States beginning on December 12, 2003. It also requires that all facilities that manufacture, process, pack or hold food for consumption in the U.S. be registered with the FDA. This registration requirement for foreign facilities is primarily enforced through the prior notice provision. The act also authorizes the FDA to detain an article of food for which there is credible evidence or information indicating such article presents a threat of serious adverse health consequences or death to humans or animals. This authority provides an added measure to ensure the safety of the nation's food supply.

Contact: U.S. Food and Drug Administration/Rules and Regulations (Prior notice Center)
Phone: Joe McCallion: 301-443-6553; Ted Poplawski: 301-443-6553;
Registration: 301-575-0156
E-mail: Ted.Poplawski@fda.gov
Website: http://www.fda.gov/oc/bioterrorism/bioact.html

C. In U.S. Waters and on U.S. Shores

National Targeting Center (NTC)

Using tools like the Automated Targeting System (ATS), Custom and Border Protection's National Targeting Center (NTC) provides tactical targeting and analytical research to support intra-departmental and inter-agency anti-terrorist operations. The

NTC also supports operations in the field, including the Container Security Initiative (CSI) personnel stationed at critical ports throughout the world.

To prevent bioterrorist attacks on the U.S. food supply, the U.S. Food and Drug Administration places personnel at the NTC to screen high risk imported food shipments and to implement provisions of the Bioterrorism Act of 2002.

Contact: Department of Homeland Security/Customs and Border Protection/National Targeting Center
Phone: 703-621-7700
Fax: 703-391-1983
E-mail: hugh.austin@dhs.gov

National Vessel Movement Center (NVMC)

About 10,000 ships make over 68,000 U.S. port calls each year. The NVMC in Kearneysville, West Virginia, receives all information regarding arrivals and departures of merchant ships in U.S. ports. This information is then categorized and forwarded to the U.S. Coast Guard's Intelligence Coordination Center and the appropriate U.S. Coast Guard Captain of the Port offices.

Contact: Department of Homeland Security/U.S. Coast Guard Intelligence Coordination Center/ Mr. Richard Harding
Phone: 202-267-6356

Sector Command Centers – Joint (SCC-J)

This joint U.S. Coast Guard and U.S. Navy initiative dates from November 2001 and exists in Norfolk, Virginia, and San Diego, California. The goal of SCC-J is to protect and defend assets within the port. It provides maritime domain awareness to deter, detect, and defend against terrorist acts. It controls access to Maritime Critical Infrastructure, Key Assets, and Military Essential Waterways.

Contact: Department of Homeland Security/Commandant, U.S. Coast Guard (G-OCC)/Mr. K. Peterson
Phone: 757-638-2763

COASTWATCH

The U.S. Coast Guard Intelligence Coordination Center, co-located with the Office of Naval Intelligence at the National Maritime Intelligence Center in Suitland, Maryland, established COASTWATCH, a process that analyzes the 96-hour Notice of Arrival reports using law enforcement and intelligence information and reporting vessels of interest so that the U.S. Coast Guard and other agencies could appropriately respond to board those vessels before they reached port, if necessary. The U.S. Coast Guard continues this practice today and has improved electronic sharing of notice of arrival reports and accompanying intelligence information with Customs and Border Protection (CBP), Transportation Security Administration (TSA), Information Analysis and Infrastructure Protections (IAIP) Directorate, Department of Defense, and other components of the Intelligence Community.

At the NMIC, the U.S. Navy's Office of Naval Intelligence brings military and civilian employees into a single command to provide "one-stop shopping" for national level maritime intelligence. The NMIC also hosts the Marine Corps Intelligence Activity (MCIA) and the Coast Guard Intelligence Coordination Center (ICC) and the Naval Information Warfare Activity (NIWA).

Contact: Department of Homeland Security/U.S. Coast Guard Intelligence Coordination Center/LT J. Dietrich
Phone: 301-669-4463

NMIC Senior Watch Officer: 301-669-2613

Maritime Intelligence Fusion Centers

Located in Norfolk, Virginia, and Alameda, California, these units compile, synthesize and distribute intelligence products from the federal, state, and local levels dealing with maritime security to homeland security officials across the country responsible for securing U.S. ports and waterways.

Contact: Department of Homeland Security/Commandant, U.S. Coast Guard (G-OCC)/Mr. K. Peterson
Phone: 757-638-2763

Operation Port Shield
www.uscg.mil/hq/g-m/mp/mtsa.shtml

Operation Port Shield implements and enforces the security requirements of the Maritime Transportation Security Act (MTSA) of 2002. Under this verification program, the U.S. Coast Guard inspects every foreign vessel, at sea or at the dock, during its initial visit to the United States and thereafter, using a Risk Based Decision Targeting Matrix. Foreign vessels calling upon the U.S. must comply with requirements set forth in the International Ship and Port Facility Security (ISPS) Code. Furthermore, the U.S. Coast Guard inspects domestic waterfront facilities which receive foreign vessels subject to the ISPS Code for security compliance with ISPS. Additionally, vessels calling upon the United States from foreign ports in non-compliant countries are subject to a series of graduated and increasingly severe restrictive actions to ensure they do not pose a security risk. U.S. Coast Guard program officers also visit foreign countries to evaluate antiterrorism measures in place at ports abroad.

Contact: Department of Homeland Security/U.S. Coast Guard/LT Craig Toomey
Phone 202-267 0476
Fax: 202-267-0506
E-mail: cstoomey@comdt.uscg.mil

Automatic Identification System (AIS)
www.uscg.mil/hq/g-m/mp/mtsa.shtml

An AIS is navigation equipment installed on ships that automatically sends the ship's identity, position, course, speed, navigational status, and other safety-related information to other ships and shore-based agencies, allowing for ship tracking and monitoring by Vessel Traffic Systems (VTS) located in various U.S. ports. The International Convention for the Safety of Life at Sea (SOLAS) Chapter V requires carriage of AIS on all ships of 300 gross tonnage and upwards engaged on international voyages, cargo ships of 500 gross tonnage and upwards not engaged on international voyages, and all passenger ships irrespective of size.

Contact: Department of Homeland Security/U.S. Coast Guard/LT Craig Toomey
Phone: 202-267-0476
Fax: 202-267-0506
E-mail: cstoomey@comdt.uscg.mil
Website: http://www.uscg.mil/hq/g-m/mp/mtsa.shtml

Area Maritime Security Committees

The U.S. Coast Guard has established committees in all the nation's ports to coordinate the activities of all port stakeholders, including other federal, state and local agencies, industry and the boating public. These groups collaborate on plans to secure their ports and pool resources to deter, prevent and respond to terror threats.

Contact: Department of Homeland Security/U.S. Coast Guard/CDR Tina Burke
Phone: 202-267-4143
Email: tburke@comdt.uscg.mil
Contact: Mr. Ike Eisentrout
Phone: 202-267-0895
Email: beisentrout@comdt.uscg.mil

Port Security Assessment Program

Under this program, the U.S. Coast Guard is examining the key infrastructure in the nation's 55 most economically and strategically important ports for potential vulnerabilities. In addition, the U.S. Coast Guard is creating a system to display key port information in an electronic geospatially referenced format to serve as a database that can be easily searched for national, regional and local information. This information will be available to port officials across the country to help them make decisions about how to reduce vulnerability of their ports.

Contact: Department of Homeland Security/U.S. Coast Guard/G-MPP-3/CAPT Tim Mann
Phone: 703-418-6609
Fax: 703-418-6764
E-mail: tmann@comdt.uscg.mil

Port Security Grants
www.portsecuritygrants.dottsa.net

The Port Security Grants Program provides federal resources for projects to enhance facility and operational security for critical national seaports. The funds assist ports in analyzing vulnerabilities and then closing gaps in security through physical enhancements like access control gates, fencing, lighting and advanced communication and surveillance systems. The program also funds security strategies that prevent and respond to terror threats.

E-Mail: portsecuritygrants@dhs.gov
Web Site: https://www.portsecuritygrants.dottsa.net

Non-Intrusive Inspection Technology (NII)

U.S. Customs and Border Protection uses NII technologies to screen a larger portion of the stream of commercial traffic in less time while facilitating legitimate trade. CBP officers use large-scale gamma ray and x-ray imaging systems to screen conveyances for contraband, including weapons of mass destruction. Inspectors also use personal radiation detectors to scan for signs of radioactive materials, as well as high-tech tools such as density meters and fiber-optic scopes to peer inside suspicious containers.

Contact: Department of Homeland Security/Customs and Border Protection/Office of Field Operations
Phone: 202-344-1180
Fax: 202-344-1435

Operation Drydock

Under this program, the U.S. Coast Guard and the Federal Bureau of Investigation work to prevent use of merchant mariner credentials by terrorists and criminals. The U.S. Coast Guard has strengthened its background checking process for commercial seamen and has begun using more tamper-resistant credentials.

Contact: Department of Homeland Security/Customs and Border Protection/Office of Field Operations
Phone: 202-344-1376

Transportation Workers Identity Credential (TWIC)

The goal of the TWIC program is to develop a secure and uniform credential to prevent potential terrorist threats from entering sensitive areas of our transportation system. When implemented, the TWIC will ensure that credentials contain a biometric identifier to authenticate identities of TWIC holders. By having one universally recognized credential, workers avoid paying for redundant cards and background investigations to enter secure areas at multiple facilities. The prototype phase is being conducted at 26 facilities in six states including the transportation facilities in the Delaware River Basin area, the Los Angeles and Long Beach area, and 12 major port facilities in the state of Florida. Up to 75,000 transportation workers are expected to participate in the prototype test. The prototype is funded with $55 million from the Transportation Security Administration's budget.

E-Mail: credentialing@dhs.gov

APPENDIX C: INTERNATIONAL, REGIONAL AND INDUSTRY ORGANIZATIONS

Working with and through international organizations that are involved in the maritime sector is critical in the effort to ensure the security of U.S. interests in the Maritime Domain through an enhanced global maritime security framework. Working with regional and industry organizations is also a major component of U.S. efforts with regard to maritime security. The following is a listing of some important maritime and international commerce related international, regional, and industry organizations, along with explanations of missions and contact information. An understanding of the missions and value of these organizations is important in achieving effective and coordinated outreach regarding U.S. maritime security policies.

D. International Organizations

Multilateral Export Control Regimes

There are four major non-proliferation regimes through which the U.S. government encourages multilateral efforts to address the threat of terrorism or proliferation of weapons of mass destruction: the Australia Group (www.austrliagroup.net), which deals with chemical and biological weapons; the Missile Technology Control Regime (www.mtcr.info/english); the Nuclear Suppliers Group (www.nuclearsuppliersgroup.org); and the Wassenaar Arrangement (www.wassenaar.org), which focuses on controls on conventional arms and dual-use exports.

International Association of Marine Aids to Navigation and Lighthouse Authorities (IALA)
http://site.ialathree.org

The International Association of Marine Aids to Navigation and Lighthouse Authorities is a non-governmental association bringing together services and organizations concerned with the provision or maintenance of marine aids to navigation systems and allied activities, at sea and on inland waterways. The aim of IALA is to foster the safe, secure, economic and efficient movement of vessels, through improvement and harmonization of aids to navigation and vessel traffic services worldwide and other appropriate means, for the benefits of the maritime community and the protection of the environment.

International Atomic Energy Agency (IAEA)
www.iaea.org

The International Atomic Energy Agency (IAEA) is the world's center of cooperation in the nuclear field. It was set up as the world's "Atoms for Peace" organization in 1957 within the United Nations family. The Agency works with its Member States and multiple partners worldwide to promote safe, secure and peaceful nuclear technologies. The IAEA's mission is guided by the interests and needs of Member States, strategic plans and the vision embodied in the IAEA Statute. Three main pillars - or areas of work - underpin the IAEA's mission: Safety and Security; Science and Technology; and Safeguards and Verification. IAEA may be contacted at Official.Mail@iaea.org, or by phone at the New York City United Nations Liaison Office at 212-963-6010.

International Labor Organization (ILO)
www.ilo.org

The International Labor Organization is the UN specialized agency which seeks the promotion of social justice and internationally recognized human and labor rights. It was founded in 1919 and is the only surviving major creation of the Treaty of Versailles, which brought the League of Nations into being. The ILO became the first specialized agency of the United Nations in 1946. The ILO maintains a branch office in Washington. It can be contacted by email at washington@ilo.org and by phone at 202-653-7652.

International Maritime Organization (IMO)
www.imo.org

The International Maritime Organization is a specialized agency of the United Nations. The IMO is responsible for measures to improve the safety and security of international shipping and to prevent marine pollution from ships. It also is involved in legal matters, including liability and compensation issues and the facilitation of international maritime traffic. Since 1959, IMO has instituted several conventions, including the International Convention for the Safety of Life at Sea (SOLAS), International Convention for the Prevention of Pollution from Ships (MARPOL), the International Management Code for the Safe Operation of Ships and for Pollution Prevention (the ISM Code), and the Convention for the Suppression of Unlawful Acts Against the Safety of Maritime Navigation (SUA). In 2002, the IMO recognized the importance of comprehensive maritime security and adopted an International Ship and Port Facility Security Code (ISPS Code). As an agency of the UN, IMO currently consists of 164 member states. IMO may be contacted by emailing info@imo.org.

International Criminal Police Organization (INTERPOL)
www.interpol.int

INTERPOL acts as a police organization in support of all organizations, authorities and services whose mission is preventing, detecting, and suppressing crime. INTERPOL seeks to provide both a global perspective and a regional focus; exchange information that is timely, accurate, relevant and complete; facilitate international co-operation; coordinate joint operational activities of its member countries; and share best practices and expertise. INTERPOL acts on the basis of the articulated demands and expectations of these organizations, authorities and services, while remaining alert to developments so as to be able to anticipate future requirements. INTERPOL may be contacted internationally at cp@interpol.int, or domestically at USNCB.Web@usdoj.gov, or by phone at 202-616-9000.

World Customs Organization (WCO)
www.wcoomd.org

The WCO, officially known as the Customs Cooperation Council (CCC), is an independent intergovernmental body whose mission is to enhance the effectiveness and efficiency of Customs administrations. It is the competent global intergovernmental organization in Customs matters and has developed a number of instruments since its formal inception in 1952. The WCO currently consists of 165 member states that collectively represent 99% of all global trade. In addition to the various Conventions and International Instruments that have been promulgated by the WCO, which deal with issues such as modernization and harmonization, capacity building and integrity development in Customs administrations, the WCO has played an active role in the development of a Framework of Standards to Secure and Facilitate Global Trade, which seeks to improve the security of the global trade supply chain while at the same time improving the ability of Customs administrations to facilitate the movement of low-risk cargo. The WCO may be contacted at information@wcoomd.org.

World Trade Organization (WTO)
www.wto.org

The WTO is an international organization with 148 member nations. The main function of the WTO is to enhance global welfare by ensuring that trade flows as smoothly, predictably and freely as possible. This is accomplished through a set of trade agreements that establish legal ground-rules for international commerce. The WTO administers these agreements, provides a forum for trade negotiations, handles trade disputes, reviews trade policies, provides technical assistance and training for developing countries, and cooperates with other international organizations. The WTO may be contacted at enquiries@wto.org.

E. Regional Organizations

Port Management Association of Eastern and Southern Africa (PMAESA)
www.pmaesa.org

The Port Management Association of Eastern and Southern Africa (PMAESA) is a non-profit, non-governmental and non-political organization of port authorities in the Eastern and Southern Africa region. Membership of PMAESA ranges from the Sudan in the North to Namibia in South-West Africa, including the Indian Ocean islands and some land-locked countries. PMAESA was established in July 1973 under the auspices of the United Nations Economic Commission for Africa (ECA). The main objectives behind the establishment of the Association are to coordinate and standardize African port operations, equipment and services of ports, with a view to improving relations with other transport organizations, sub-regionally or world-wide. In addition, PMAESA provides a forum for its members to share experiences, exchange views on common problems and how best to address them, and on matters of interest to all the Association's members. PMAESA may be contacted at pmaesa@africaonline.co.ke

Organization of American States (OAS)
www.oas.org

The Organization of American States (OAS) brings together the thirty-five independent countries of the Western Hemisphere to strengthen cooperation and advance common interests. The OAS works to promote good governance, strengthen human rights, foster peace and security, expand trade, and address the complex problems caused by poverty, drugs and corruption. Through decisions made by its political bodies and programs carried out by its General Secretariat, the OAS works to promote greater inter-American cooperation and understanding. OAS may be contacted by email at pimultimedia@oas.org, or by phone at (202) 458-6824.

Asian-Pacific Economic Cooperation (APEC)
www.apecsec.org.sg

Asia-Pacific Economic Cooperation (APEC) provides a forum for facilitating economic growth, cooperation, trade and investment in the Asia-Pacific region. APEC operates on the basis of non-binding commitments, open dialogue and equal respect for the views of all participants. APEC works to reduce tariffs and other trade barriers across the Asia-Pacific region. The Bogor Goals are key to achieving APEC's vision of free and open trade and investment in the Asia-Pacific region. APEC also seeks to create an environment for the safe and efficient movement of goods, services and people across borders in the region through policy alignment and economic and technical cooperation. APEC has 21 members which account for more than a third of the world's population, approximately 60% of world GDP, and about 47% of world trade. APEC may be contacted at info@apec.org, or by phone at (65) 6775 6012.

F. Industry / Trade Organizations

Baltic and International Maritime Council (BIMCO)
www.bimco.org/

Founded in 1905, BIMCO is the world's largest and most diverse private shipping organisation. Its membership spans 123 countries and includes more than 2,550 companies. Owner members alone control 65% of the world merchant fleet, while 1,500 brokers and agents and 100 club and associate members complete BIMCO's international coverage, which in some segments, encompasses 80% of the cargo carrying capacity of specific ship types. BIMCO intervenes on its members' behalf with inter-governmental organizations, and regional and national authorities, and advocates international rather than regional or national regulations. It actively participates in many International Maritime Organization (IMO) working groups and sub-committees, keeping the IMO informed of shipping's point of view on the various issues. BIMCO actively urges that uniform application and enforcement of existing international conventions and regulations is undertaken worldwide. BIMCO may be contacted by email at mailbox@bimco.dk

International Association of Drilling Contractors (IADAC)
http://www.iadc.org/

IADC is the only organization that represents the worldwide oil and gas drilling industry. Its mission is to promote commitment to safety, preservation of the environment and advances in drilling technology. Through conferences, training seminars and various publications, IADC aims to foster education and communication within the petroleum industry.

International Association of Dry Cargo Shipowners (INTERCARGO)
www.intercargo.org/

Since 1980 the International Association of Dry Cargo Shipowners (INTERCARGO) has represented the interests of owners, operators and managers of dry cargo shipping. In addition, INTERCARGO works closely with the other international associations to promote a safe, high quality, efficient and profitable industry. INTERCARGO is the sole international shipowners' association dedicated to the needs of the dry cargo industry. INTERCARGO's vision is for a safe, efficient and environmentally friendly dry cargo maritime transport industry where its members' ships serve world trade operating competitively, safely and profitably. INTERCARGO may be contacted by email at info@intercargo.org, and by phone at +44 (0)20 7977 7030.

International Association of Independent Tanker Owners (INTERTANKO)
www.intertanko.com/

International Association of Independent Tanker Owners (INTERTANKO) membership is comprised of independent tanker owners and operators of oil and chemical tankers, i.e. non-oil companies and non-state controlled tanker owners, who fulfill the Association's membership criteria. As of January 2005, the organization had 235 members, whose combined fleet comprises more than 2,230 tankers totaling 170 million deadweight[11], which is 70% of the world's independent tanker fleet. INTERTANKO's associate membership stands at 285 companies with an interest in shipping of oil and chemicals. INTERTANKO is a forum where the industry meets, policies are discussed and statements are created. It is a source of first-hand information, opinions and guidance. INTERTANKO seeks to create a professional, efficient and respected industry that is dedicated to achieving Safe transport, cleaner seas and free competition. INTERTANKO may be contacted by email at washington@intertanko.com, or by phone at the North America Office at (703) 373-2269.

International Association of Ports and Harbors (IAPH)
www.iaphworldports.org/

The International Association of Ports and Harbors (IAPH) ultimate goal is to represent Port CEOs, Port Directors and Port Managers in order to promote and advance their common cause and interests. IAPH strives to fulfill the following mission to promote the development of the international port and maritime industry by fostering cooperation among members in order to build a more cohesive partnership among the world's ports and harbors, thereby promoting peace in the world and the welfare of mankind; to ensure that the industry's interests and views are represented before international organizations involved in the regulation of international trade and transportation and that they are incorporated in the regulatory initiatives of these organizations; and to collect, analyze, exchange and distribute information on developing trends in international trade, transportation, ports and the regulations of these industries. IAPH may be contacted by email at info@iaphworldports.org.

International Chamber of Commerce (ICC)
www.iccwbo.org/

The International Chamber of Commerce (ICC) acts as the voice of world business, championing the global economy as a force for economic growth, job creation and prosperity. ICC activities cover a broad spectrum, from arbitration and dispute resolution to making the case for open trade and the market economy system, business self-regulation, fighting corruption or combating commercial crime. ICC has access to national governments all over the world through its national committees. The organization's Paris-based international secretariat feeds business views into intergovernmental organizations on issues that directly affect business operations. ICC may be contacted by email at webmaster@iccwbo.org, or by phone at +33 1 49 53 28 28.

---

[11] The term deadweight refers to the total weight (expressed in tons) of cargo, cargo equipment, bunkers, provisions, water, stores and spare parts which a vessel can lift when loaded to her maximum draught as applicable under the circumstances.

International Chamber of Shipping (ICS)
www.marisec.org/ics/index.htm

The International Chamber of Shipping (ICS) is the international trade association for merchant ship operators. ICS membership comprises national ship-owners' associations representing over half of the world's merchant fleet. A major focus of ICS activity is the International Maritime Organization (IMO), the United Nations agency with responsibility for the safety of life at sea and the protection of the marine environment. ICS is involved in a wide variety of areas including any technical, legal and operational matters affecting merchant ships. ICS is unique in that it represents the global interests of all the different trades in the industry: bulk carrier operators, tanker operators, passenger ship operators and container liner trades, including ship-owners and third party ship managers. ICS has consultative status with a number of intergovernmental bodies which have an impact on shipping. Its ties with IMO date to its inception in 1958. ICS is committed to the principle of maritime regulation being formulated at an international level. The objective of ICS is the maintenance of a sound, well-considered global regulatory environment in which well-run ships can operate safely and efficiently. ICS may be contacted via the Chamber of Shipping of America by email at info@knowships.com or by phone at (202) 775-4399.

The International Confederation of Free Trade Unions (ICFTU)
www.icftu.org/

The ICFTU was set up in 1949 and has 233 affiliated organizations in 154 countries and territories on all five continents. It has three major regional organizations, APRO for Asia and the Pacific, AFRO for Africa, and ORIT for the Americas. It also maintains close links with the European Trade Union Confederation (ETUC) (which includes all ICFTU European affiliates) and Global Union Federations, which link together national unions from a particular trade or industry at international level. It is a Confederation of national trade union centers, each of which links together the trade unions of that particular country. Membership is open to bona fide trade union organizations that are independent of outside influence, and have a democratic structure. The ICFTU cooperates closely with the International Labour Organization and has consultative status with specialized agencies such as UNESCO, FAO, etc. The ICFTU organizes and directs campaigns on issues such as: the respect and defense of trade union and workers' rights; the eradication of forced and child labor; the promotion of equal rights for working women; the environment; education programs for trade unionists all over the world; encouraging the organization of young workers; sends missions to investigate the trade union situation in many countries. The five main ICFTU priorities are: employment and international labor standards; tackling the multinationals; trade union rights; equality, women, race and migrants, and trade union organization and recruitment. The ICFTU may be contacted at internetpo@icftu.org.

International Council of Cruise Lines (ICCL)
www.iccl.org/index.cfm

The mission of the International Council of Cruise Lines (ICCL) is to participate in the regulatory and policy development process and promote all measures that foster a safe, secure and healthy cruise ship environment. Under the direction of the chief executives of its member lines, ICCL advocates industry positions to key domestic and international regulatory organizations, policymakers and other industry partners. The ICCL actively monitors international shipping policy and develops recommendations to its membership on a wide variety of issues. ICCL's members include the largest passenger cruise lines that call on hundreds of ports in the United States and abroad. ICCL Associate Members represent industry suppliers and strategic business partners. Each year ICCL's overnight cruise ship operators carry more than seven million passengers on over 90 ships. ICCL may be contacted by email at info@iccl.org, or by phone at the Arlington, VA office at (703) 522-8463.

International Federation of Customs Brokers Associations (IFCBA)
www.ifcba.org/index.htm

The International Federation of Customs Brokers Associations, commonly referred to as the IFCBA, began in 1989 when associations representing the industry in six nations Australia, Canada, Japan, Korea, New Zealand and the United States — met at the Pacific Rim Customs Brokers Conference in Hawaii. These associations established a professional international business network where the industry could strategize about future challenges. IFCBA membership currently stands at 25 countries. The IFCBA has grown into an association that is recognized by customs administrations and other regulatory authorities at the national, regional and international level. The objectives of the IFCBA are, broadly speaking, threefold: (1) to encourage and facilitate co-operation among national customs broker associations at the international level, (2) to facilitate the exchange of information and ideas on matters affecting national customs broker associations, and (3) to associate, affiliate and federate with any other association, society or organization, with the objects the same or similar to the objects of the IFCBA. IFCBA may be contacted by email at ifcba@ifcba.org, or by phone in the Washington, DC office at 202-466-0222.

International Federation of Shipmasters' Associations (IFSMA)
www.ifsma.org/

The International Federation of Shipmasters' Associations (IFSMA) was formed in 1974 by Eight European Shipmasters' Associations to unite the World's serving Shipmasters into a single professional coordinated body. It is a non-profit, apolitical organization dedicated solely to the interest of the serving Shipmaster. More than 8000 Shipmasters from more than 40 Countries are affiliated to IFSMA either through their National Associations (36) or as Individual Members (55). IFSMA is a Federation established to uphold International Standards of Professional Competence for Seafarers commensurate with the need to ensure Safe Operational Practices, Preservation from Human Injury, Protection of the Marine Environment and Safety of Life and Property at Sea. IFSMA may be contacted by email at HQ@ifsma.org, or by phone at +(44) 207 261 0450.

International Harbor Masters' Association (IHMA)
www.harbourmaster.org/

The International Harbor Masters' Association (IHMA) was founded in Reykjavik, Iceland in 1996 with more than 250 members in 52 countries worldwide. Membership encompasses almost 80 nations and extends throughout Western and Eastern Europe, Australia, Africa, the Americas, the Middle East and Asia. Membership consists of harbormasters from ports large and small, publicly and privately owned, and represents a unique source of up-to-date, hands-on expertise in a range of maritime operations. The objectives of IHMA are to: promote the safe, secure and environmentally sound conduct of marine operations in port waters; develop and foster collaboration and good relations among harbor masters world-wide; represent the professional views of harbor masters internationally, regionally and nationally; promote the professional standing and interests of harbor masters generally; collect, collate and supply information of professional interest to the membership and to provide any other service to the membership that may be deemed appropriate. IHMA may be contacted by email at secretary.ihma@harbourmaster.org, or by phone at +44 1329 832771.

International Maritime Pilots Association (IMPA)
www.impahq.org/

International Maritime Pilots' Association (IMPA) is a professional, nonprofit body with an international outlook. It is primarily concerned with promoting professional standards of pilotage worldwide in the interests of pilots' safety. It seeks to fulfill this task by encouraging both consultation between its members and the exchange of technical information with other industry partners and regulators at the local, national and international levels. To date, it has some 8,000 members in well over 40 countries. IMPA may be contacted by email at secgen@impahq.org, or by phone at +(44) 20 7240 3973.

International Parcel Tankers Association (IPTA)
http://www.ipta.org.uk/

International Parcel Tankers Association (IPTA) serves to further the interests of member companies while promoting better relations in or affecting the bulk liquids cargo industry. IPTA cooperated for many years with the European Coastal Chemical Tankers Organization – ECCTO – and as a result of the recognition of their common interests a joint secretariat was established in 1998. IPTA, recognized as an international organization with expertise in the specialized parcel/chemical tanker field, was granted consultative status as a Non-Governmental Organization to the IMO in 1997. IPTA members are committed to the enhancement of Maritime Safety and the protection of the Marine Environment. IPTA may be contacted by email at mail@ipta.org.uk, or by phone at (44) 1524 - 811 892.

International Ship Managers' Association (ISMA)
www.isma-london.org/index.htm

The idea behind ISMA at its foundation in 1991 was to improve standards in ship management and achieve a safer, more environmentally conscious, more reliable, and more controllable ship management industry. This continues to be the goal of the Association. As an association, ISMA represents the views of its members in international organizations such as IMO and European Union and groups such as BIMCO. ISMA acts as a forum for the exchange of information among members, and promotes both the Association and its members on the basis of their pursuit of quality not only within the shipping industry, but also with insurers, port and flag states and the press. ISMA's mission: establish and maintain the ISMA Best Practice Guidelines as the leading tool for ship managers; encourage the highest standards in ship and crew management through innovation, creativity, and the sharing of knowledge amongst its members; provide a forum for discussion on matters of common interest to the ship and crew management industries; and promote the interests of ship and crew management industries in general. ISMA may be contacted by email at secretary@isma-london.org, or by phone at +44 (0) 1403 733070.

International Shipping Federation (ISF)
www.marisec.org/isf/index.htm

ISF is a broad based international employers' organization dedicated to maritime manpower issues. In the plethora of international organizations, ISF represents the employer, explaining employers' activities to the media. To others, ISF is an authority on the STCW Convention and assists with advice on its detailed technical requirements. Externally, ISF has consultative status with the International Labor Organization (ILO), and with the International Maritime Organization (IMO). ISF reviews United States developments through links with a Washington office and attends, through ILO, meetings of the Paris Memorandum of Understanding on Port State Control Committee. ISF, with national shipowner association members from Eastern and Western Europe, the Indian Sub-Continent, the Asia/Pacific Region, the Middle East and North, Central and South America, provides a forum for employers to co-ordinate effectively and influence events on maritime human resources issues. ISF is the sister organization of the International Chamber of Shipping (ICS). ISF may be contacted via the Chamber of Shipping of America by email at info@knowships.com or by phone at (202) 775-4399.

International Tanker Owners Pollution Federation (ITOPF)
www.itopf.com

The International Tanker Owners Pollution Federation (ITOPF) is a non-profit organization, involved in all aspects of preparing for and responding to ship-source spills of oil and chemicals in the marine environment. ITOPF was established after the Torrey Canyon incident[12] to administer the voluntary compensation agreement, TOVALOP, which assured the adequate and timely payment of compensation to those affected by oil spills. TOVALOP came to an end on February 20, 1997. ITOPF now devotes considerable effort to a wide range of technical services, of which the most important is responding to spills of oil and chemicals. Other services ITOPF provides include damage assessment, contingency planning, training and information. ITOPF may be contacted at central@itopf.com, or by phone at +44 (0) 20 7566

International Transport Workers' Federation (ITF)
www.itfglobal.org/

The International Transport Workers' Federation (ITF) is an international trade union federation of transport workers' unions. 624 unions representing 4,400,000 transport workers in 142 countries are members of the ITF. It is one of several Global Federation Unions allied with the International Confederation of Free Trade Unions (ICFTU). The aims of the ITF are: to promote respect for trade union and human rights worldwide; to work for peace based on social justice and economic progress; to help its affiliated unions defend the interests of their members; to provide research and information services to its affiliates; and to provide general assistance to transport workers in difficulty. Although the range of ITF activities is very wide, they can be best summed up under three key headings: representation, information, and practical solidarity. The ITF represents the interests of transport workers' unions in bodies which take decisions affecting jobs, employment conditions or safety in the transport industry, such as the International Labour Organisation (ILO), the International Maritime Organisation (IMO) and the International Civil Aviation Organisation (ICAO). The ITF may be contacted at mail@itf.org.uk.

Society of International Gas Tanker and Terminal Operators (SIGTTO)
www.sigtto.org/

The Society of International Gas Tanker and Terminal Operators (SIGTTO) is the international body established for the exchange of technical information and experience, between members of the industry, to enhance the safety and operational reliability of gas

---

[12] In March 1967 the tanker TORREY CANYON wrecked on the south coast of England, discharging her entire cargo of crude oil into the English Channel. This incident focused international attention on the problem of massive oil pollution resulting from tanker incidents. Source: Pollution Incidents In and Around U.S. Waters A Spill/Release Compendium: 1969 - 2001 - U.S. Coast Guard

tankers and terminals. To this end the Society publishes studies and produces information papers and works of reference for the guidance of industry members. It maintains working relationships with other industry bodies, governmental and intergovernmental agencies, including IMO, to promote the safety and integrity of gas transportation and storage schemes. SIGTTO may be contacted by email at secretariat@sigtto.org, or by phone at +44 (0) 20 7628 – 1124.

World Nuclear Transport Institute (WNTI)
www.wnti.co.uk/index.html

The World Nuclear Transport Institute (WNTI) was established in 1998 to promote sound and objective principles for ensuring radioactive materials are transported safely, efficiently and reliably within a secure international framework. WNTI is the only body dedicated to presenting the industry point of view on radioactive materials transport from an international perspective. WNTI is a global industrial organization for all sectors of the radioactive materials transport industry. WNTI is active on an international level where the views and interests of industry need to be represented, in particular, intergovernmental organizations such as the International Maritime Organization (IMO) and the International Atomic Energy Agency (IAEA) which play a key role in establishing standards and regulations that apply to radioactive materials transport. WNTI may be contacted by email at wnti@wnti.co.uk, or by phone in the North America office at (202) 785-8101.

World Shipping Council (WSC)
www.worldshipping.org/index.html

The World Shipping Council is a Washington, D.C.-based trade association representing more than forty liner shipping companies serving America's international trade. Council members include the largest container lines in the world as well as smaller niche carriers, and carriers providing roll-on/roll-off and heavy-lift services. In addition to ocean transportation, they provide a wide range of intermodal and logistics services to American importers and exporters. The Council's goal is to provide a coordinated voice for the liner shipping industry in its work with policymakers and other industry groups interested in international transportation issues, including: maritime security, regulatory policy, tax issues, safety, the environment, harbor dredging and upgrading the infrastructure needed to handle America's booming trade. The World Shipping Council may be contacted by email at info@worldshipping.org, or by phone at (202) 589-1230.

The National Strategy for Maritime Security

The Maritime Infrastructure Recovery Plan

Maritime Transportation System Security Plan

National Plan to Achieve Maritime Domain Awareness

Domestic Outreach Plan

The Maritime Commerce Security Plan

Global Maritime Intelligence Integration Plan

International Outreach and Coordination Strategy

Maritime Operational Threat Response Plan

Appendix D: Acronyms and Definitions

Acronym	Definition
AMS	Area Maritime Security
DHS	Department of Homeland Security
DOS	Department of State
DOT	Department of Transportation
FACA	Federal Advisory Committees Act
GMIIP	Global Maritime Intelligence Integration Plan
HSAC	Homeland Security Advisory Council
HSPD	Homeland Security Presidential Directive
ICCO	Interagency Coordinating Committee for Outreach
IT	Information Technology
MCS	Maritime Commerce Security
MDA	Maritime Domain Awareness
MSPCC	Maritime Security Policy Coordination Committee
MSWG	Maritime Security Working Group
MTS	Marine/Marine Transportation System
NSMS	National Strategy for Maritime Security
NSPD	National Security Presidential Directive